Thank you for today

Thank you
for today

Table Of Contents

Foreword

The world today is full of uncertainties and challenges, and the last thing that we want to do is to say "thank you". With the hardships, turmoil, difficulties and problems that people are facing these days, it really becomes even harder to see the good sides of the world. Things become so irrational and unpredictable. The world becomes so different. Being grateful in this very ungrateful world is really challenging.

However, one must understand that although the world seems so difficult and things might go the way you want it to be, there are still many things to be grateful for. No matter what good things happen in your life, if you don't have the attitude of gratitude, you will never be completely happy.

Learning to be grateful when things go wrong, when problems strike, when difficulties happen will make a huge difference in your life and the way you will feel about life itself. Life is always better once you feel blessed no matter how difficult things might seem.

Gratitude is seeing life as a great and wonderful gift. Once you feel great about the world and about your life, you will find real happiness and peace.

When everything goes wrong, it is really hard to be in the state of gratitude, but if you remain thankful about even those little blessings you have, your life will become happier. Learning to be grateful in this ungrateful world is something worth doing.

Get all the info you need here.

Gratitude for Today
Learning to Be Grateful In An Ungrateful World

Chapter 1:

Introduction

Synopsis

Developing an attitude of heartfelt and sincere Gratitude for all your current blessings unleashes the ultimate power for obtaining many more. Give thanks each day and you will see how being grateful for everything you have today can create great changes in your life.

"Thank you" – these two simple words can change one's life. With the problems that we may face every day in our lives, these two little words are often the most neglected words each day. We always see the worst in life that is why we never become truly happy.

Expressing your gratitude or even being thankful about the things you have is really important. This will change your entire life - the way you see life, the way you handle your problems and the way you cope with the daily challenges.

What does Gratitude Means?

Gratitude means counting your blessings, thankfulness, acknowledging things that you receive and noticing those simple pleasures in your life. The moment you wake up in the morning, say a little prayer, giving thanks to another life given to you. Gratitude means learning to live a kind of life as if things were miracles, and it also means being fully aware on continuous bases about how much you have been given.

Gratitude also shifts your focus from the things you lack in life towards great abundance that is now present. It is also good to note that psychological and behavioral research has shown the most amazing improvements in life brought by the practice of gratitude. Bring thankful and appreciating life and the things life offers you makes us more resilient and even happier.

Resilient in the sense that no matter what challenges and difficulties we experience, we know that life is not cruel to give us something that we can't bear. It gives us strength with the belief and the mindset that no matter how many problems we may encounter, the blessings we receive are much greater than them. Gratitude strengthens relationships, reduces stress and improves health.

Chapter 2:

Synopsis

Once you develop an attitude of a sincere attitude for all the blessing you receive, this unleashes the power for you to receive even more than you already have.

Having the feeling of gratitude essentially means taking nothing for granted and giving thanks about the abundance in life that you have obtained. Gratitude actually fits in with abundance in various aspects. As a famous writer says, " A lot of people are trapped in the state of poverty by having lack of gratitude." Abundance always goes with gratitude because we can always attract great wealth as well as abundance with the power of gratitude.

How It Fits

The word "thank you" means a lot of things and these are actually the most perfect words that you have to say for just everything. Many people today are wondering why their life is not really abundant, why many good things don't happen to them, why aren't they completely happy. There are a lot of "whys".

Many people are living in a life full of complaints. This is actually one of the main reasons behind your lack of abundance in life. If you always see things negatively, you will never appreciate the good things you possess and the blessing you receive.

Once you start looking at everything in your life as a blessing and as good things to be grateful for, then your life will become meaningful and you will be happy. Your sense of gratitude will bring great abundance that you have been dreaming of. The way you see life, the way you think about the things around you, make a huge difference about how abundant you are in your life today.

The feeling of gratitude is really powerful and it an essential part of your life that has the ability to bring yourself to the things you want. When you start looking and focusing your own energy on being truly grateful, you bring real abundance in your life.

Life is full of blessings. It is filled with a lot of things that you need and you desire. We just really complicate it with our negative thought patterns. Once you open your eyes for the best things around you and for all the simple things that can be great for you, you can see how rich you are and how abundant your life really is. Gratitude always fits in with abundance. They primary key towards obtaining real abundance in life is through learning to become grateful even in though you are living in an ungrateful world.

Chapter 3:

Deciding What To Be Grateful For

Synopsis

There are a lot of things around us to be grateful for; it's just a matter of appreciating the blessing you receive and acknowledging how blessed you for having them. Educating yourself for the feeling of attitude actually means taking nothing for granted and giving value to whatever you posses. Practice the attitude of never putting off n action or the word for the expression of your gratitude.

Many individuals tend to take for granted the things that are present in their lives. There is actually a gratitude exercise instructing us to imagine losing few of the things that you are taking for granted today such as your family, your home, as well as your ability to hear and see, to walk or just anything that is currently giving you comfort.

Imagine losing them and then imagine that you are getting each of them back every day. Think how thankful you would be when it happens and when each one is given back to you.

Deciding

Starting finding happiness even in those small things you posses rather than holding out for great and big achievements like getting job promotion, having a baby or getting married. There are a lot of things to be grateful for.

When you wake in the morning, be thankful for the life you have for another day. Your happiness always depends on how you view life itself and how you see your life today. If you begin to think that there are much more things to be grateful for, you will see how happy your life will is.

If you want to fully appreciate life and your existence, you have to be really mindful about even those little things around you. A butter that flies around you that make you feel good, the food on your table, your good health – these things might be very simple for you, but if you begin to acknowledge them as blessings, your life will become happier.

Use gratitude in order to guide you in putting things in their right perspective. If everything around you seems wrong, and if things do not go the way you want them to be, bear in mind that in every problem and difficulty carries inside it the seeds of a greater benefit.

When you are facing any challenge in your life and when you are in the face of great adversity, just ask yourself about the good things that you can get from it. Understand how you can benefit from a certain situation.

When you begin to appreciate life and even the small things that may happen to you, you also begin to create a life of happiness, harmony, contentment and bliss. If you are experiencing a difficult situation, never think of it as a burden or a punishment. Be thankful about the trials that you are facing because they can make you even stronger. Be grateful for your problems because they make you a better individual.

Chapter 4:

How Gratitude Works With Abundance

Synopsis

Gratitude is something that does not require any explanation; everyone knows how to become grateful. As being said, gratitude is about appreciating everything you receive and counting your blessings. However, there are a lot of people who don't really know that gratitude great works with abundance. Gratitude and abundance go mutually. Although you may not know it, but it is actually true that your feeling of gratitude always brings abundance. This actually brings you even more of what you really appreciate.

How It Works

Gratitude speeds together with the manifestations of the things that you want. Gratitude attracts what you really want. As the universal Law of Attraction reveals, we can attract into our lives the things that we focus on and we think about.

Now, once you're consciously aware of the things you receive and you are grateful for receiving them, you're also focusing clearly on those that you want in life and you are attracting even more of those things to your life.

You have to remember that gratitude is really powerful. This is in fact a really strong emotional energy that one must be able to project in the manner of manifesting their wants in life.

If you are thankful about the things you receive and the blessings in your life, you are attracting abundance. Providing emphasis on a feeling of gratitude towards whatever life offers you immediately bring you into an energetic alignment having an increased abundance.

Gratitude is what really keeps you stay connected to great power. Also, the more you learn and practice being appreciative and thankful, there will more thought patterns of real gratitude that you build in your own subconscious. Eventually, you are resonating with the higher level of energy and be able to attract more good things into your life.

Gratitude perfectly works with obtaining great abundance. If you're in a heartfelt gratitude state, your vibrational resonance is more powerful. You begin to resonate, thereby, you project an even higher vibrational frequency that exactly attracts you to those conditions, circumstances and event that you want.

If you are in the state of gratitude, you begin in to count your blessings. You are beginning to determine the good things around you and you disregard the negativities surrounding you. If you begin to be happy and contented with whatever you have in life, you easily acknowledge even the simple blessings you receive.

With this, you are not only being abundant temporally with the riches you want, but you are also able to receive amazing blessing beyond your comprehension. Your life becomes happier, you experience peace of mind, you improve the quality of your life – which serves as the greatest abundance you can have in your life.

Chapter 5:

Getting In The Right Mindset

Synopsis

Having the right mindset means finding something to be grateful for in every difficulty. If you have the set way of thinking about life and the things around you, you are able to see the opportunity behind every problem. If you are able to acknowledge the good things in your life amidst diversity, you have the right mindset that will lead you towards a happy life.

In the face of difficulties and in today's sinking economy, it is really difficult to us to remain appreciative and grateful. Once you feel overwhelmed and stressed out, it is sometimes hard to find reasons to become grateful. It is true that most of the times, finding the good in difficult situation can really be challenging.

However, the great benefits of maintaining appreciation and genuine gratitude in spite of what is going on around you, are truly worth looking into. Having the right mindset about being grateful and appreciative can greatly transform your life.

The Mindset

Learn to Count your Blessings

Each of us has our own blessings in life. Regardless of who you are, where you came from, or what you are going through, you always have blessings in your life that you can be grateful for. The only challenge here is to educate yourself to provide emphasis on gratitude and search for many reasons in order for you to manifest appreciation.

Practice to Acknowledge the Good

If you are a type of person who is not really appreciative, well this is the best time for you to develop your new habit. This habit is about searching for something to be thankful for about every situation, experience that you encounter or person.

In every difficult situation that you encounter, this can really be difficult, but if you are able to develop this habit, you can see significant changes in your life and how you view life itself. You just have to work hard in finding a little piece of diamond in a huge rocky mountain.

You can also give thanks for a loving relationship with your partner and family, your good health and those positive outcomes in various situations.

Gratitude is really powerful and being fully aware of the blessings you receive can have huge impacts on your life. If you are filled with thankfulness and appreciation, this change your reality's dynamic.

Genuinely express appreciation and gratitude for those people around you. If something good happen to you, no matter how big or small it is, be thankful that it happens.

If you get into the right mindset about having a feeling of gratitude towards others and each situation, you will also feel good about yourself. You will have a different perspective about life and you will view the world as something beautiful.

It is truly amazing how a positive action can create so much change in the life of a person. Acknowledging the great power of attitude is actually one of the most important things today that create a great effect on one's life. In very tangible ways, it is true that gratitude can make your life even better.

Chapter 6:

Synopsis

Your way of thinking about gratitude, whether positive or negative, can create different impacts in your life. There are great differences in positive and negative mindset in gratitude, and whatever your way of thinking about it can make significant changes in the quality of your life. Gratitude always matters. If you have a negative mindset in gratitude, you will see difficulty in each opportunity, but if you have positive mindset in gratitude, you can see great opportunities in each difficulty.

The Good And The Bad

Negative Mindset in Gratitude

All people receive blessings – in any way or in any form. The problem is that most people don't really appreciate them or even take these blessings for granted. People often forget to offer regular thanks for what they already obtained. Nowadays, it is usually easier to just slip into the negative mindset and focus more on your bigger goals for the future and to those things that you have yet to achieve.

Well, there is actually nothing wrong with aiming high and looking upwards and onwards; this is part of human nature. However, the problem with it is that you starting to forget the current blessings that you are obtaining.

If you have a negative mindset in gratitude, you will not totally be happy. If you start taking for granted the things that you already have because of your bigger objectives, you will become frustrated and you will obtain real happiness, especially if you are still far from your objectives.

If you are able to recognize even the simple things around you, while aiming to reach your goal, there is actually great difference between these two. You can aim for higher goals while acknowledging the things you already have today.

Positive Mindset in Gratitude

The words you speak and the feeling you express everyday greatly affect your life. If you are obtaining great joy and abundance in life, it is also because of how you think about the things around and the words you speak. If you have a positive mindset in gratitude, you give more appreciation to even the smallest things around you, and because of this, you become even happier.

The way you think about gratitude and your attitude towards the things around you have great impacts in your life. Bear in mind that a positive energy given out will eventually return with great rewards.

The way you think about gratitude reflects in the way you see life. Remember that gratitude is of your most important connection to God, expressing your appreciation for the good things in your life and in return, obtaining even more for you to be thankful for. Give appreciation to everything around you and you will also attract joy and abundance in your life.

Chapter 7:
Turning Bad Days Into Gratitude Days

Synopsis

When things don't go our way and when everything around us seems to fall apart, the last thing that we can think of is to be thankful. When we are facing difficulties, all we do is complain and ask why bad things are happening to us. Turning bad days into gratitude days is really a great challenge for many people, but it is always possible.

Practice Counting your Blessings – Not all your Troubles

People spend most of their time lamenting about their troubles, complaining about the difficulties they suffer from that they no longer care about the blessings that they have received. When faced in difficulties, people really tend to forget what they have and the good things in their life.

People are all invited to start counting their blessings, even name them one by one and they will just be surprised about those amazing things that God had done into their lives. When faced in trials and adversities, count your blessings and you will also see that you heart will grow warmly with much feelings of gratitude as well as sweet feelings of happiness and peace.

Look at the Brighter Side of Every Situation

If you experience problems and difficulties at work, be more grateful that you have your own work. If you are facing challenges in life, be more grateful of these challenges because due to them, your life is not boring.

If you are facing trials in your life today, be thankful that these can give you much strength to overcome more trials in the future. Appreciate your challenges in life that can help you learn and be a stronger person.

To say that we are grateful does not mean that everything in your life is perfect; it only means that you are aware of all your blessings in spite of the challenges that you are experiencing.

 If you remain angry, upset and frustrated because you are having a really bad day, that won't change anything. In fact, that would make things worse.

Bring grateful during these times can brighten up your day as well as others. Getting what you want is not the only reason for you to grateful, sometimes, your appreciation in life becomes even more valuable when you learn to be appreciative in times of troubles and difficulties.

If you are in a difficult situation, instead of hating the world for giving you such problem, think of the benefit that you can benefit from it. Think about the things that you can gain from this situation and through this, you will become more inspired to overcome the difficult situation you are into.

Always look for something to be grateful for in every bad day you face. Also, it is better to understand the reason you are in such situation and think of the best things that you can obtain from it. If you learn to become more grateful and happy with every situation you are in, you can become happier in your life.

Always be grateful that you do not already have all the things that you want because if you did, there will be nothing more to look forward to. Be more grateful for every difficult satiation you are into because in those times, you are able to grow.

Chapter 8:

How Gratitude Can Change What you Attract

Synopsis

Being grateful in any kind of situation is really a powerful and strong attracting force. Gratitude reduces negativity, helps people learn, improves relationships and most importantly, gratitude attracts that things that you want. This is a great and powerful force that can change what one is able to attract.

The Great Power of Gratitude

Once you find things you appreciate and you start providing emphasis on the things you are thankful for, you can always attract them. As you start flooding your mind with gratitude or appreciation, you actually attract more of those that you want. If you are in a state of gratitude, you are also in a high energy vibration essential in attracting more things that you can be thankful for. There will also be more things that will magically come to you – things that are actually drawn into you by your focus and great feelings of gratitude.

Getting What You Want

To simply An emotion of happiness attracts the conditions of happiness and in the same way, your feeling of appreciation attracts more things that you can be grateful for. In the Universal Law of Attraction, it actually reveals that one will attract into their life the things that they focus on and think about.

If you express your gratitude towards something, then you are fully aware of that blessing. In this case, you're providing more focus on the things that you really want in life and thus, you are attracting more of these things into your own life.

Also, gratitude makes the things that you want more tangible and serves as real aspect of your reality. The more real and tangible your desires are, the more you will provide great focus on them. As being said, gratitude is really powerful. It can resolve problems, improves your life, helps you learn and attract the things that you want.

This can greatly change what you attract because the more aware you are about the blessings and good things you receive, you give more focus to it by expressing your appreciation. This will in turn enables you to attract positive energies to obtain what you want.

Gratitude really matters. It does not only allow us to obtain what we want but it also leads to positive actions. When one feels grateful for the kindness showed by a person, one may be more likely to show kindness in the person in return. This is then really helpful in creating good relationships with others.

With many blessings that you can take benefit from appreciation and giving thanks on the things you receive, there is no reason for you not to the practice the attitude of gratitude. This will not only attract good things on your life but on the lives of others as well.

Chapter 9:

Advantages And Disadvantages

Synopsis

Gratitude unleashes life's fullness. Living a life full of gratitude can always make you happy and at peace. There are a lot of advantages that you can think of once you start showing your gratitude towards other people. Also, appreciating your life brings great benefits that can actually increase the quality of your life.

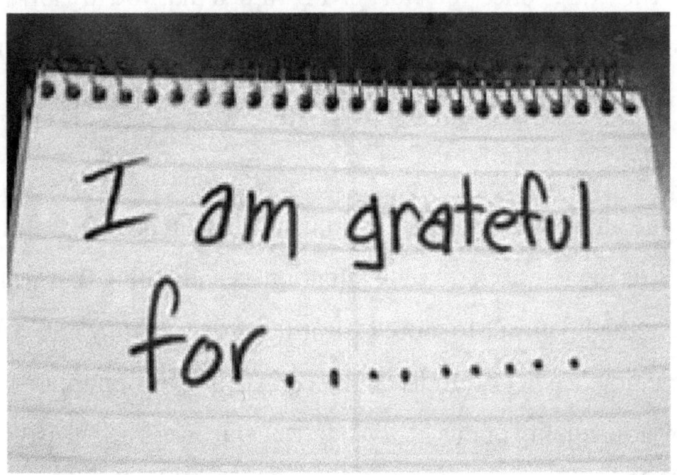

The Differences

Advantage of Gratitude

Gratitude can remind us of the positive and great things in our lives. It can make us happy, knowing that in every difficult situation that we are facing, there are still a lot of things to be thankful for. If you practice an attitude of gratitude, you can always turn your bad days into good days. Gratitude is also really advantageous because it can remind us of what is important. It is hard to whine or complain about some little things once you start giving things that you are alive today and healthy. It is also difficult to be overwhelmed or stressed out on your over paying bills once you are happy and grateful that you have a home with your family.

Gratitude allows us to see the world in a beautiful perspective. It enables us to view each difficult situation as something that will give us strength and power to more forward and live a happy and colorful life. The practice of gratitude can increase our level of happiness and improve the quality of our life. When you start viewing the world as a beautiful place for you to learn, improve yourself and become stronger, your life becomes more meaningful.

Once you are able to recognize the things that you must be thankful for, you will also discover that you are starting to appreciate simple things and pleasures that you formerly took for granted. Gratitude is something that shouldn't be only a reaction in order to get what you want or attract what you desire, but it must be something that can help you acknowledge those little things around you. This must also be something that can help you constantly search for the good though unpleasant situations may happen.

Most of the times, when talking about negative situation, we believe that it is harmful, sad, difficult and even stressful. However, if you have an attitude of gratitude, you are able to think positively in each negative situation. You look into each detail and try to find something to be grateful for. You believe that there is something good in every difficult situation and problems are seen as opportunities to improve yourself and to grow.

Disadvantage of Gratitude

With the said great advantages of gratitude, one could hardly find anything wrong about showing your gratitude and appreciation to every situation and every person. Gratitude is something that will always bring the peace, contentment and happiness to people. It has the ability to reduce negativities, improve all relationships, attract what your heart desires, and bring happiness to one's life.

Gratitude is free. It requires no money and just a little time so there is no excuse for anyone to show how much they appreciate an individual or give thanks to any situation they are in. With the positive characteristics of gratitude, it is really hard for anyone to find any disadvantage about it.

Conclusion

Gratitude is really a powerful emotion. It unveils the fullness of one's life and it can turn negative things into something beautiful. Gratitude can turn chaos into order, denial to acceptance and confusion into clarity. It can turn a house to a home, a stranger to a friend and it create a life worth living.

Gratitude must not only be an expression after you have received something you want; but it must also be something that can help you search for opportunities to be grateful for even during unpleasant situations. Now, start bringing the attitude of gratitude into your own experiences and rather than waiting for positive outcomes for you to feel grateful.

In times of difficult situations, find something to be grateful for. Everything happens for a reason and in every problem, there is always something good that you can get. If you have been complaining about the kind of life you have, then this is the right time to take a pause, think and look for the good things in whatever situation you are in. Start living a life of gratitude.

If you haven't say "thank you" to a friend because of a simple tap when you are facing problems in your life, this is the perfect time for you to show your appreciation to him or her. Be thankful for your ability to see, to hear, to smell, to talk and to walk. Count your blessings and you will certainly be surprised about how many blessings you have been receiving throughout your life. Speak of words of gratitude and see how you can attract the things you want in life. Recognize all your achievements and also give thanks to yourself for keeping strong. Give thanks to your parents, a simple "thank you" note will do.

Have you done something good to others but never received any token of appreciation? Not even the word "thank you". If you feel disappointed with that, think about how disappointed your parents are for not receiving even just a word of thanks for the lunch they packed, things they bought and dinner prepared for you.

If things don't go your way, and you think that there is nothing to be grateful for, just seek for something good out of such situation. If you don't have all the things that you want, then be thankful because if you do, there will be nothing more to look forward to.

Be grateful for all your imperfections because they provide you an opportunity to improve more. Be grateful for every challenge you face because it can build your character. Don't despair if you commit mistakes because your mistakes will teach you important lessons. Always be grateful. Show your gratitude to everyone and to every situation and you will see how it can change the quality of your life.